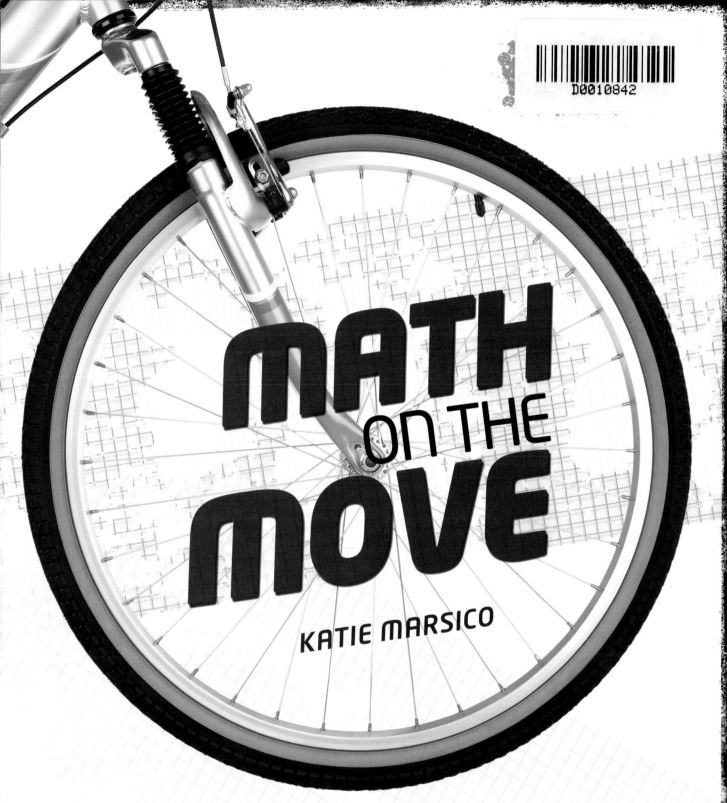

MATH ON THE MOVE

KATIE MARSICO

Lerner Publications Company • Minneapolis

To Stephanie Pecoraro, a sweet girl and Maria's
dear friend and fellow math student

Lerner Publications Company
A division of Lerner Publishing Group, Inc.
241 First Avenue North
Minneapolis, MN 55401 USA

For reading levels and more information, look up this title at www.lernerbooks.com.

Photo Acknowledgments
The images in this book are used with the permission of: © iStockphoto.com/Don Nichols, p. 1; © iStockphoto.com/rusmor, p. 1 (background); © Image Source/Getty Images, p. 4; © iStockphoto.com/spxChrome, pp. 5, 9, 13, 17, 19, 25, 27 (notebook); © iStockphoto.com/DNY59, p. 5 (map); © iStockphoto.com/alubalish, pp. 5, 9, 15, 19, 25, 27 (torn paper); © Ronnie Kaufman/Blend Images/Getty Images, p. 6; © iStockphoto.com/fotosjcm, p. 7 © gbh007/iStock/Thinkstock, p. 8; © Py2000/Dreamstime.com, p. 9; © iStockphoto.com/jwebb, p. 10; © Riccardo_Mojana/iStock/Thinkstock, p. 11; © Fuse/Thinkstock, pp. 12, 24; © hypnotype/Shutterstock.com, p. 13; © Bruce Laurance/Blend Images/Thinkstock, p. 14; © iStockphoto.com/GP232, p. 15; © iStockphoto.com/izusek, p. 16; © iStockphoto.com/mbbirdy, p. 17 (clock); © iStockphoto.com/Okea, p. 17 (jet); © Margot Petrowski/Shutterstock.com, p. 18; © iStockphoto.com/chapin31, p. 19; © Jupiterimages/Stockbyte/Thinkstock, p. 20; © aboikis/Shutterstock.com, p. 21; © Per Breiehagen/Iconica/Getty Images, p. 22; © iStockphoto.com/Icepparo, p. 23; © Baloncici/Dreamstime.com, p. 25; © Alex Mares-Manton/Asia Images/Getty Images, p. 26; © Flame of life/Shutterstock.com, p. 27; © iStockphoto.com/monticelllo, p. 28; © iStockphoto.com/inhauscreative, p. 29.

Front cover: © iStockphoto.com/grandriver; © iStockphoto.com/rusmor (background).
Back cover: © iStockphoto.com/suprun.

Main body text set in Conduit ITC Std 14/18. Typeface provided by International Typeface Corp.

Library of Congress Cataloging-in-Publication Data

Marsico, Katie, 1980–
        Math on the move / by Katie Marsico.
            pages   cm — (Math everywhere!)
        Includes index.
        ISBN 978–1–4677–1882–0 (lib. bdg. : alk. paper)
        ISBN 978–1–4677–4696–0 (eBook)
        1. Length measurement—Juvenile literature. 2. Distances—Measurement—Juvenile literature. 3. Mathematics—Juvenile literature. I. Title.
        QC102.M373 2015
        530.8—dc23   2013049792

Manufactured in the United States of America
1– CG — 7/15/14

TABLE OF CONTENTS

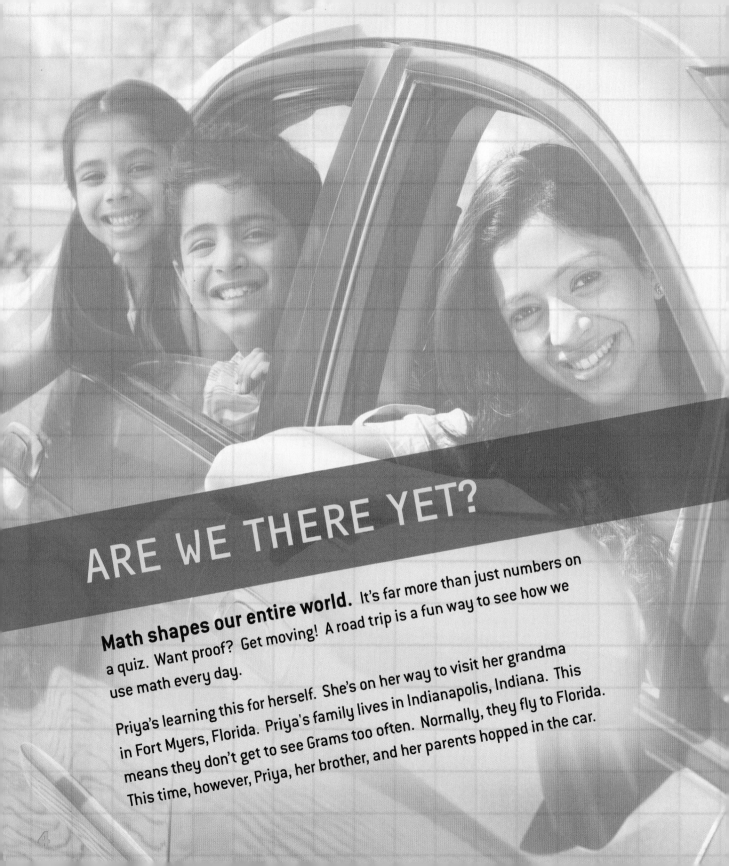

ARE WE THERE YET?

Math shapes our entire world. It's far more than just numbers on a quiz. Want proof? Get moving! A road trip is a fun way to see how we use math every day.

Priya's learning this for herself. She's on her way to visit her grandma in Fort Myers, Florida. Priya's family lives in Indianapolis, Indiana. This means they don't get to see Grams too often. Normally, they fly to Florida. This time, however, Priya, her brother, and her parents hopped in the car.

Today was their first day on the road. Altogether, they spent a little less than seven hours on the road. Tonight they're checking into a hotel.

Priya's enjoying the drive. She and her brother have been reading and playing games in the car. She's starting to get impatient, though. How much farther before they hit the Sunshine State? Her dad tells her to hold tight. The distance between Indianapolis and Fort Myers is 1,108 miles (1,783 kilometers).

Dad says they're about one-third of the way there. So far, they've moved at a good pace. He hopes to continue covering the same distance each day.

How many more miles to go before they reach Fort Myers? Round to the nearest mile. How many total days will Priya spend on the road, including the trip home?

DO THE MATH!

Suppose you're taking the same road trip as Priya. Your family even plans to drive the same distance each day. Along the way, you'll stop in Atlanta, Georgia. It's about halfway between Indianapolis and Fort Myers. You leave Indianapolis early Saturday morning. About how far away is Atlanta? What day will you arrive there?

Check your answers to all math problems on pages 30–31.

CRUISING THROUGH CALIFORNIA

Pablo and his Aunt Ali enjoy a mini-vacation every summer. The past few years, they've driven to Monterey, California. Pablo loves to hike and kayak there. Monterey is 341 miles (549 km) north of Pablo's hometown. The drive usually takes about five and a half hours.

Distance ÷ time = miles per hour (mph).

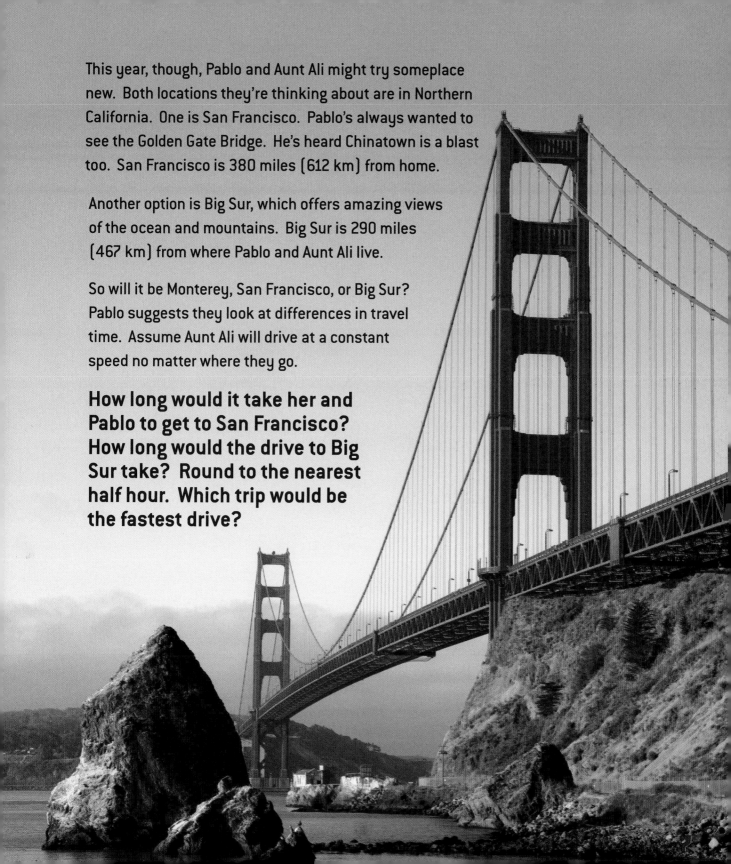

This year, though, Pablo and Aunt Ali might try someplace new. Both locations they're thinking about are in Northern California. One is San Francisco. Pablo's always wanted to see the Golden Gate Bridge. He's heard Chinatown is a blast too. San Francisco is 380 miles (612 km) from home.

Another option is Big Sur, which offers amazing views of the ocean and mountains. Big Sur is 290 miles (467 km) from where Pablo and Aunt Ali live.

So will it be Monterey, San Francisco, or Big Sur? Pablo suggests they look at differences in travel time. Assume Aunt Ali will drive at a constant speed no matter where they go.

How long would it take her and Pablo to get to San Francisco? How long would the drive to Big Sur take? Round to the nearest half hour. Which trip would be the fastest drive?

BIKE OR BUS?

Who needs a bus when there's a bike path next to your yard? That's how Jacob felt last year. He still lived at his old house then. Jacob could bike the 0.5 miles (805 meters) between home and school in three minutes.

But Jacob's family moved over the summer. Luckily, his new house is along the same bike path. Yet it's also about 1 mile (1.6 km) farther away from school.

Jacob's new home is on the bus route, as well. In fact, the bus stops right on the corner. That's just one house over from Jacob's. The driver picks everyone up at 7:55 a.m. She makes only one other stop. So Jacob would get to school in about 10 minutes.

Assume Jacob bikes at the same speed he did last year. The bell rings at 8:10 a.m. **Should he bike or ride the bus if he wants a few extra minutes to sleep in?**

DO THE MATH!

Let's say today is a late-arrival day at your school. That means buses will run one hour and five minutes behind schedule. It's a five-minute walk from your house to the bus stop. If you're super short on time, you can run the distance in about three minutes. The bus normally picks you up at 7:47 a.m. This morning, you leave home at 8:48 a.m. Can you stroll to the bus stop? Or should you sprint to play it safe?

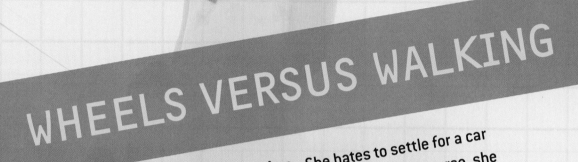

WHEELS VERSUS WALKING

Kiley's all about being active. She hates to settle for a car ride when she could zoom around on her skateboard! Of course, she never leaves home without her helmet. Kiley also loves walking. She's always up for a brisk stroll in the fresh air.

This afternoon, Kiley's going to the park. Softball practice starts at 1:30 p.m. Until then, she's keeping a close eye on the clock. She's also deciding how she wants to travel.

Kiley moves pretty fast on her skateboard. She hasn't officially clocked her speed. But Kiley usually skates to her friend Avi's house in 15 minutes. She walks there in 30 minutes.

Kiley's and Avi's houses are 2 miles (3.2 km) apart. The distance between Kiley's home and the park is 0.8 miles (1.3 km).

How much time should Kiley set aside to skate to practice? How long would it take if she wants to walk?

Kiley would rather be a little early than a little late. Play it safe by rounding up to the next whole minute!

HOW MANY MUSEUMS?

Farewell, Windy City! Well, almost. It's 9:30 a.m., and Meg and her dad are wrapping up a visit to Chicago, Illinois. They have a million more sights to see before heading back to Michigan tonight. Their train leaves at 6:00 p.m. The ticket agent said to be at the station 30 minutes before their scheduled departure.

Meg and her dad decide to focus on Chicago's Museum Campus. They plan to visit the natural history museum and the aquarium. If there's time left over, it would be cool to tour the planetarium, as well.

Dad guesses it's a 10- to 15-minute cab ride between the campus and their hotel. An online map says it's only a one-minute walk from the museum to the aquarium. The stroll from the aquarium to the planetarium is approximately six minutes. Dad estimates that they'd probably spend an hour and a half at each location.

They know they'll also need to set aside an hour for lunch. And they have to factor in a 10- to 15-minute cab ride back to their hotel. Then it'll take roughly 30 minutes to gather their luggage and check out.

Meg wants to eat dinner at the restaurant down the street. She'd like to visit a few local stores too. Dad says they should give themselves two hours to dine and shop. Finally, there's one last 10- to 15-minute cab ride to the train station. **Do Meg and her dad have enough time for the museum, the aquarium, *and* the planetarium?** To be safe, plan on 15 minutes for each cab ride.

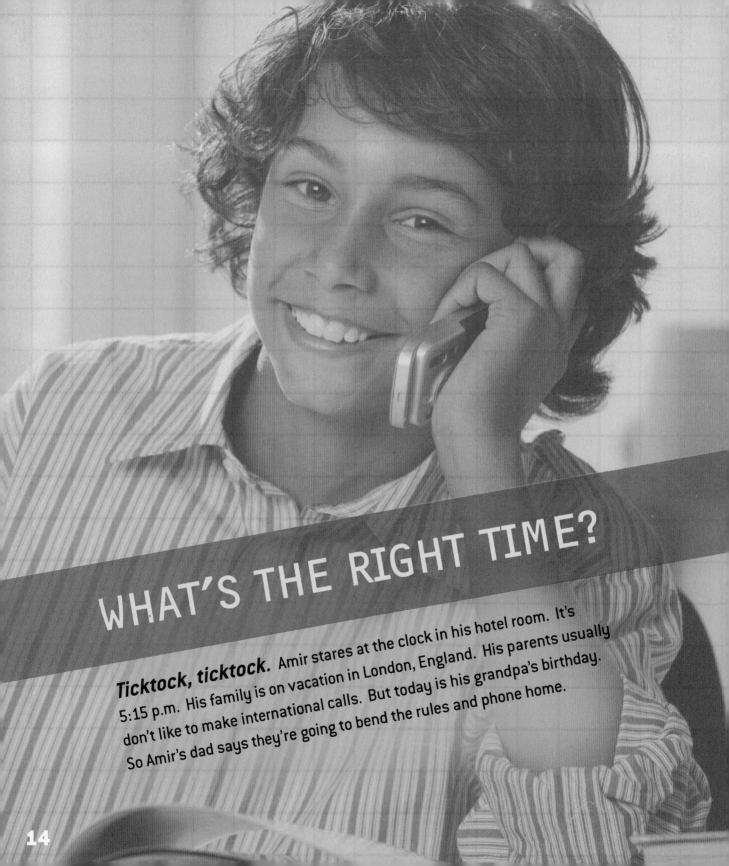

WHAT'S THE RIGHT TIME?

Ticktock, ticktock. Amir stares at the clock in his hotel room. It's 5:15 p.m. His family is on vacation in London, England. His parents usually don't like to make international calls. But today is his grandpa's birthday. So Amir's dad says they're going to bend the rules and phone home.

Amir is ready to start dialing! But Dad tells him to hold on. He reminds Amir that Grandpa lives in Oregon. That means he's in a different time zone than anyone in London. It's eight hours later in England than it is in Oregon.

Besides, Grandpa doesn't get home from his morning workout until 11:00 a.m. That's *Grandpa's* time, of course.

How much longer should Amir wait to call? What time will it be in London when he finally sings "Happy Birthday"?

DO THE MATH!

Set your alarm, soccer star! Picture yourself playing for a traveling soccer team in Nebraska. Tomorrow, you have a game in Lincoln at 2:45 p.m. Your mom thinks it'll take about five hours to get there. You live in Sidney. That's in the western part of the state. It's also in a different time zone. Sidney is one hour behind Lincoln. Normally, you shower and dress in 30 minutes. You eat breakfast in about 10 minutes. Then you usually spend 15 minutes walking the dog. When should you plan to wake up tomorrow?

CATCH THE CONNECTING FLIGHT!

Thank goodness for rolling suitcases! Nika and her mom have to hustle to make their connecting flight. They're traveling from Boston, Massachusetts, to Houston, Texas. But Nika's mom didn't book a direct flight. So they have a brief layover in St. Louis, Missouri.

Their flight out of Boston took off at 8:52 a.m. The pilot predicted they'd be in the air two hours and 34 minutes. She also reminded everyone that St. Louis is one hour behind Boston.

Unfortunately, they ran into a few thunderstorms. As a result, the plane landed 19 minutes late. It was another 15 minutes before passengers could disembark. The plane to Houston leaves at 11:11 a.m. The next flight to Houston doesn't take off until 4:52 p.m.

Nika and her mom just set foot inside the airport. **How much time do they have to catch their connecting flight? If they're not fast enough, how long will they be in St. Louis?**

HEAD OUT ON THE HIGHWAY?

Kay's swim team usually meets at the local pool. But this weekend, they're competing in a different location. This pool is in a suburb about 10 miles (16 km) east of Kay's town. Her older brother Mike offers to drive her. Kay says she'll look up directions online. Meanwhile, Mike listens to the traffic report on TV.

The website lists two different routes. One route is mostly on the highway. The other uses only local roads. Kay prints both sets of directions. Then she hurries downstairs to find Mike. Along the way, she glimpses the clock. Whoops! It's later than she thought.

Kay tells Mike they'd better get going. She suggests taking the highway. The speed limit for most local roads is only 30 miles (48 km) per hour. And the pool is right next to the highway exit ramp.

Normally, Mike would agree with her. The speed limit on the highway is 55 miles (89 km) per hour. But Mike just heard that there's a backup. The traffic reporter mentioned a 15-minute delay along the stretch of highway they'd be traveling.

Which option is a better bet if Kay wants to be on time to her meet?

Remember that 1 hour = 60 minutes.

And again, it's better to be cautious. Round up to the next whole minute when comparing travel times!

DO THE MATH!

Your mom is driving to your tennis match. She's taking the highway. The exit ramp Mom needs to use is 5.4 miles (8.7 km) from the court. Unfortunately, she zooms right past it! The next exit is 4.6 miles (7.4 km) away. Then she'll have to backtrack 3.1 miles (5 km) on local roads. The speed limit on those roads is 30 miles (48 km) per hour. Luckily, Mom says she's only five minutes from the next exit. You need to be on the court at 12:15 p.m. It's 11:58 a.m. Will you make it?

A LONG WAY TO BROADWAY

Sean's ready for a song other than "The Wheels on the Bus." His class is taking a bus from Montclair, New Jersey, to New York City. They're going to see a Broadway play!

Before they left, Sean asked his teacher how far they'd be driving. Ms. Lin said it was 16 miles (26 km) from their school to the theater. At first, the bus moved pretty quickly. But then Sean spotted some signs along the highway. They said: "Road construction ahead. Expect delays!" Sure enough, traffic slowed to a crawl.

It's 1:15 p.m. Sean spies the speedometer. They're moving at about 25 miles (40 km) per hour. The driver tells Ms. Lin they're 8 miles (13 km) from the theater. They still have 7 miles (11 km) to go on the highway.

The show starts at 2:00 p.m. Suppose the bus doesn't speed up until it exits the highway. Then it takes the driver another five minutes to get to the theater. **Will Sean and his class arrive before the curtain rises?**

DON'T SNOOZE AND LOSE!

Who gets the airplane window seat? Dad lets Deb have it. They're flying from Salt Lake City, Utah, to Phoenix, Arizona, for a wedding.

After takeoff, Dad suggests playing "I Spy." Deb thinks he's gone crazy. What besides clouds can you see from a plane window?

Well, the Grand Canyon, for one! Dad says they'll probably be able to spot a hole that size, even from thousands of feet above the ground. So Deb keeps her eyes peeled.

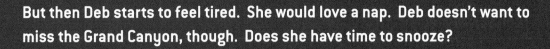

But then Deb starts to feel tired. She would love a nap. Deb doesn't want to miss the Grand Canyon, though. Does she have time to snooze?

Probably! Dad thinks they can estimate when they'll pass over the canyon. Before takeoff at 8:30 a.m., the pilot made an announcement. He said they'd be flying 507 miles (816 km) in one hour and eight minutes. He mentioned it would take 15 minutes to climb higher and higher into the sky. By then, they'd be about 95 miles (153 km) outside of Salt Lake City. Then the plane would begin moving at a constant speed of 500 miles (805 km) per hour.

Dad and Deb read an in-flight brochure. It says the Grand Canyon is 181 miles (291 km) from where they'll be landing. It's 8:45 a.m.

How far away is the Grand Canyon from their current location? How long can Deb doze?

Remember that she'd rather cut her nap short than snooze through sightseeing. And Deb can't set the timer on her watch to fractions of a minute. So round her nap time down to the nearest whole minute.

OUT-OF-TOWN EXPENSES

Duffel bag? Check! Skates? Check! Wallet? Wait . . . Gino needs to chat with his parents about that one. His hockey team has a big out-of-town game Saturday morning. No one wanted to hit the road before dawn. So Coach Ed and some parents offered to make the trip Friday instead.

They'll leave right after school and stay in a hotel overnight. Gino will be home early Saturday evening. Meanwhile, he's figuring out travel expenses.

First, there's the hotel. Three boys can sleep in a single room. The rate for the room is $109 a night, including tax. Gino also needs money for meals. And he'd like to have a few extra dollars handy. You never know when you'll need ice cream!

Gino's parents hand him $50. His dad tells him to give whatever's left over to Coach Ed. After all, gas isn't cheap!

During his trip, Gino eats out three times. On Friday, he pays $3.89 for dinner. The next day, breakfast and lunch cost a total of $7.08. After the game, the team stops for sundaes. Luckily, Coach Ed treats.

How much gas money can Gino offer him?

DO THE MATH!

Your friend's dad is driving you and your friends to an amusement park. Like Gino, you want to help with travel costs. So you calculate gas expenses. The park is 38 miles (61 km) away. Your friend's dad drives a minivan. It's similar to your mom's car. Mom tells you her minivan uses 1 gallon (3.8 liters) of gas for every 28 miles (45 km). The local gas station charges about $3.22 a gallon. What will your friend's dad spend on fuel for the entire trip? Start by figuring out how much gas is needed to drive to the park. Then calculate the cost. When you're done, determine the price of fuel for the entire distance. Round to the nearest cent.

25

WHICH WAY TO WASHINGTON?

Care to visit the Capitol? The student council is planning a day trip to Washington, DC. It was Josh's idea. He's the treasurer. His friend Mina is the president. The council hopes to cover transportation costs for all the third graders. There are 35 third graders.

Eight parents and teachers have volunteered to go along. They're willing to pay for themselves. But Principal Davis says the school will help with their travel expenses.

Josh knows there's $50.25 in the treasury. The council may have to do some fund-raising. But first, they need to price travel options. Josh checks out train tickets to Washington. The class would be departing from Baltimore, Maryland. Round-trip tickets cost $14 per person. The school offers to cover the adults' train fares.

Meanwhile, Mina researches driving costs. All eight adults are willing to drive. Five own minivans and sport-utility vehicles (SUVs). Each of those holds seven people, including the driver. The other three chaperones have sedans. A sedan has room for four people besides the driver.

The school would cover gas expenses if the adults drive. So driving seems cheaper. Yet Mina still has to think about parking fees. She phones two garages. One is $10 per vehicle for one day. But Mina learns this garage is often full. The other is $20 per vehicle for a day. It's usually less crowded. Mina decides to play it safe. She figures out the total cost for each garage.

Would the class need to use all eight cars? Will driving cost less than the train? Remember that you only need to calculate the costs for the students' fares. Assume the student council picks the cheaper travel option. **How much fund-raising must they do?**

DO THE MATH!

Splash! Want to view Baltimore from the water? The city's water taxi service is a cool way to travel. It's a boat that takes people across Baltimore's Inner Harbor. You use the water taxi every other month. Your parents ride with you. So do your two brothers. They're one and six. You're nine years old. An all-day pass is $12.50 for anyone 11 or older. It's $6.50 if you're three to 10 years old. Someone younger than three rides free. People can also buy a yearly family pass for $250. It's good for four passengers. This pass covers an unlimited number of rides for 12 months. Is it a better deal for your family to get the yearly pass or individual tickets?

READY, SET, TRAVEL!

Are you ready to show off your new math skills on a road trip? Don't jump into the car just yet. You have a few final problems to tackle.

Grab your Mickey Mouse ears! Your family is planning a 10-day trip to Disney World. The trip will begin on a Saturday and end on a Monday. You'll need to get from Milwaukee, Wisconsin, to Orlando, Florida, and back again. The question is, should you fly or drive to reach Mickey's doorstep?

Your mom says the main issues to think about are money and time. Either way, you'll have to eat three meals a day and sleep in hotels at night. So, she tells you not to focus on food or lodging right now.

There are four people in your family. That means you'd need to buy four round-trip plane tickets. Each costs $375.60. If you drive instead, you'd have to pay for gas. The distance from Milwaukee to Orlando is 1,253 miles (2,017 km). Your dad says the family car uses 1 gallon (3.8 L) of gas for every 25 miles (40 km) it's driven. The current price of gas is $3.27 per gallon.

How does the cost of driving compare with the cost of flying? Round to the nearest penny.

If you fly, you'll be in Orlando 10 days. Most direct flights take two hours, 19 minutes. Your parents would prefer to arrive in Orlando no later than 5:00 p.m.

What should your latest departure time be? Remember, Florida's time is an hour ahead of Wisconsin's.

If you drive, your parents want to leave first thing Saturday morning. They'd like to cover about 375 miles (604 km) a day. **If you stick to that schedule, when would you get to Orlando? When would you need to leave Disney World to return home on time?**

Answer Key

Page 5   There are 739 miles (1,189 km) still to drive. (⅓ of the total distance × 1,108 mi. = 369 mi.; 1,108 mi. − 369 mi. = 739 mi.)
Priya will spend a total of six days on the road. (1,108 mi. × 2 trips = 2,216 mi.; 2,216 mi. ÷ 369 mi./day = 6 days) (1 day × 3 = 3 days one way; 3 days × 2 trips = 6 days)

Do the Math!
Atlanta is about 554 miles (892 km) away. (½ of the total distance × 1,108 mi. = 554 mi.)
You'll arrive there on Sunday. (554 mi. ÷ 369 mi./day = 1.5 days; 1.5 days from Saturday morning = Sunday afternoon)

Page 7   It would take Aunt Ali and Pablo about six hours to get to San Francisco. (341 mi. ÷ 5.5 hrs. = 62 mph.; 380 mi. ÷ 62 mph. = 6.1 hrs.)
It would take them about 4.5 hours to get to Big Sur. (290 mi. ÷ 62 mph = 4.7 hrs.)
Driving to Big Sur would be the fastest trip.

Page 9   Jacob should bike. (0.5 mi. ÷ 3 min. = 0.17 mi./min.; 1 mi. + 0.5 mi. = 1.5 mi.; 1.5 mi. ÷ 0.17 mi./min. = 8.8 min., or about 9 min.; 8:10 a.m. − 9 min. = 8:01 a.m.; 8:01 a.m. = later than 7:55 a.m.)

Do the Math!
You should sprint. (7:47 a.m. + 1 hr. and 5 min. = 8:52 a.m.; 8:52 a.m. − 8:48 a.m. = 4 min.; 4 min. < 5 min.)

Page 11   Kiley would need seven minutes to skate to practice. (2 mi. ÷ 15 min. = 0.13 mi./min.; 0.8 mi. ÷ 0.13 mi./min. = 6.2 min., or about 7 min.)
It would take her 12 minutes to walk. (2 mi. ÷ 30 min. = 0.07 mi./min.; 0.8 mi. ÷ 0.07 mi./min. = 11.4 min., or about 12 min.)

Page 13   Meg and her dad don't have enough time for all three places. (15-min. cab ride + 90 min. at the museum + 1 min. walk + 90 min. at the aquarium + 6 min. walk + 90 min. at the planetarium = 292 minutes for the Museum Campus; 60 min. lunch + 15 min. cab ride + 120 min. dinner and shopping + 30 min. luggage and checkout + 15 min. cab ride = 240 min. for activities after the Museum Campus; 292 min. + 240 min. = 532 min.; 532 min. ÷ 60 min./hour = 8 hours 52 min.; 9:30 a.m. + 08:52 = 6:22 p.m., which is past the train departure time)

Page 15   Amir should wait another hour and 45 minutes to call. (5:15 p.m. − 8 hrs. = 9:15 a.m.; 11:00 a.m. − 9:15 a.m. = 1 hr., 45 min.)
It will be 7:00 p.m. in London when he sings "Happy Birthday." (5:15 p.m. + 1 hr., 45 min. = 7:00 p.m.)

Do the Math!
You should wake up by 7:50 a.m. tomorrow. (2:45 p.m. − 1 hr. = 1:45 p.m. Sidney time; 1:45 p.m. − 5 hrs. = 8:45 a.m. to leave home; 30 min. + 10 min. + 15 min. = 55 min.; 8:45 a.m. − 55 min. = 7:50 a.m.)

Page 17   They have 11 minutes to catch their connecting flight. (8:52 a.m. + 2 hrs., 34 min. = 11:26 a.m.; 11:26 a.m. − 1 hr. = 10:26 a.m.; 10:26 a.m. + 19 min. = 10:45 a.m.; 10:45 a.m. + 15 min. = 11:00 a.m.; 11:11 a.m. − 11:00 a.m. = 11 min.)
If they miss the flight, they'll be in St. Louis for five hours and 41 minutes. (4:52 p.m. − 11:11 a.m. = 5 hrs., 41 min.)

Page 19 The route using local roads should be faster. (10 mi. ÷ 55 mph = 0.18 hrs.; 0.18 hrs. × 60 min. per hr. = about 11 min.; 11 min. + 15 min. = 26 min.; 10 mi. ÷ 30 mph = 0.33 hrs.; 0.33 hrs. × 60 min. per hr. = 20 min.; 20 min. < 26 min.)

Do the Math!
You should make it. (3.1 mi. ÷ 30 mph = 0.1 hrs.; 0.1 hrs. × 60 min. per hr. = 6 min.; 6 min. + 5 min. = 11 min.; 11:58 a.m. + 11 min. = 12:09 p.m.; 12:09 p.m. < 12:15 p.m.)

Page 21 Sean and his class should arrive before the curtain rises. (7 mi. ÷ 25 mph = 0.28 hrs.; 0.28 hrs. × 60 min. per hr. = 16.8 min. or about 17 min.; 17 min. + 5 min. = 22 min.; 1:15 p.m. + 22 min. = 1:37 p.m.)

Page 23 The Grand Canyon is 231 miles (372 km) away. (507 mi. – 181 mi. = 326 mi.; 326 mi. – 95 mi. = 231 mi.) Deb can doze for 27 minutes. (500 mi./hr. ÷ 60 min. = 8.3 mi./min.; 231 mi. ÷ 8.3 mi./min. = 27.8 min. or about 27 min.)

Page 25 Gino can offer Coach Ed $2.70. ($109 ÷ 3 boys = $36.33/boy; $3.89 + $7.08 = $10.97; $36.33 + $10.97 = $47.30; $50 – $47.30 = $2.70)

Do the Math!
Your friend's dad will spend $9.02 on fuel for the entire trip. (38 mi. ÷ 28 mi./gal. = 1.4 gal.; 1.4 gal. × $3.22/gal. = $4.508; $4.508 × 2 trips = $9.02)

Page 27 The class would need only seven cars. (35 students + 8 adults = 43 people. 5 minivans/SUVs × 7 people = 35 people; 43 people – 35 people in the SUVs/minivans is 8 people in sedans; 8 people ÷ 5 people/sedan = 1.6 or 2 sedans)
Driving would cost less than the train. (35 students × $14 = $490; $10 × 7 cars = $70; $20 × 7 cars = $140; $490 > $70; $490 > $140)
The class must earn either $19.75 or $89.75, depending on which parking garage they use. ($70 – $50.25 = $19.75; $140 – $50.25 = $89.75)

Do the Math!
It's a better deal for your family to get individual tickets. ($12.50 × 2 adults = $25; $6.50 × 2 kids = $13; $25 + $13 = $38; $38 × 6 times/year = $228; $228 < $250)

Page 29 **Ready, Set, Travel!**
The cost of driving is $1,174.75 less than the cost of flying. (1,253 mi. × 2 trips = 2,506 mi.; 2,506 mi. ÷ 25 mi./gal. = 100.2 gal.; 100.2 gal × $3.27 = $327.65; $375.60 × 4 plane tickets = $1,502.40; $1,502.40 – $327.65 = $1,174.75)
Your latest departure time should be 1:41 p.m. (5:00 p.m. – 1 hr. = 4:00 p.m.; 4:00 p.m. – 2 hrs., 19 min. = 1:41 p.m.)
You'd get to Orlando on Tuesday. (1,253 mi. ÷ 375 mi./day = 3.3 days; 3.3 days from Saturday = Tuesday)
You'd need to leave Disney World on Friday to return home on time. (3.3 days before Monday = Friday)

Glossary

departure: leaving a location to travel to another

disembark: to leave a plane or a ship

estimate: to calculate without using exact numbers or information

fare: the fee a person pays to use public transportation

layover: a waiting period between two flights that are part of the same journey

route: the path someone uses to get from one place to another

speed: the rate at which someone travels

speedometer: a device on a vehicle that displays the vehicle's speed

time zone: a region where everyone uses a common standard time

Further Information

IXL Math: Third Grade
http://www.ixl.com/math/grade-3
This site includes examples and practice problems to help you perfect your growing math skills.

Thielbar, Melinda. #3 *The Secret Ghost: A Mystery with Distance and Measurement.* Minneapolis: Graphic Universe, 2010.
In this graphic novel, Sam and Michelle use measuring tools and calculations to figure out the truth about the creepy old house their dad just bought.

Travel Math
http://www.travelmath.com
This site provides quick travel calculations and will be a handy resource as you plan your next trip!

Woodford, Chris. *Distance.* New York: Gareth Stevens Publishing, 2013.
Check out this title for extra math problems involving distance.

Index